WORDS UNSAID

WORDS UNSAID

By Jony Larrowe

An Aspen Woman's Poetry and Art
Over Seven Decades

Edited by Marjorie DeLuca

PHOTOS

© 2024, Estate of Jony Larrowe, Greg Poschman, executor
Printed in the United States of America

ISBN 978-0-9991218-6-3

Book editing, design and production by Marjorie DeLuca
Aspen Graphic Solutions • info@aspengfx.com

"Trees" cover art by Jony Larrowe

Contents

Contents (cont.)

For Words Unsaid

This glorious day,
this special mood
have slipped away,
unpursued.
The heartfelt phrase,
the gracious word,
the simple praise
have gone unheard.

Then, why withhold
the golden flow?
Must we grow old
before we know…
not to wait
to appreciate?

—*Jony Larrowe*

(First appeared in Denver Post, 1963)

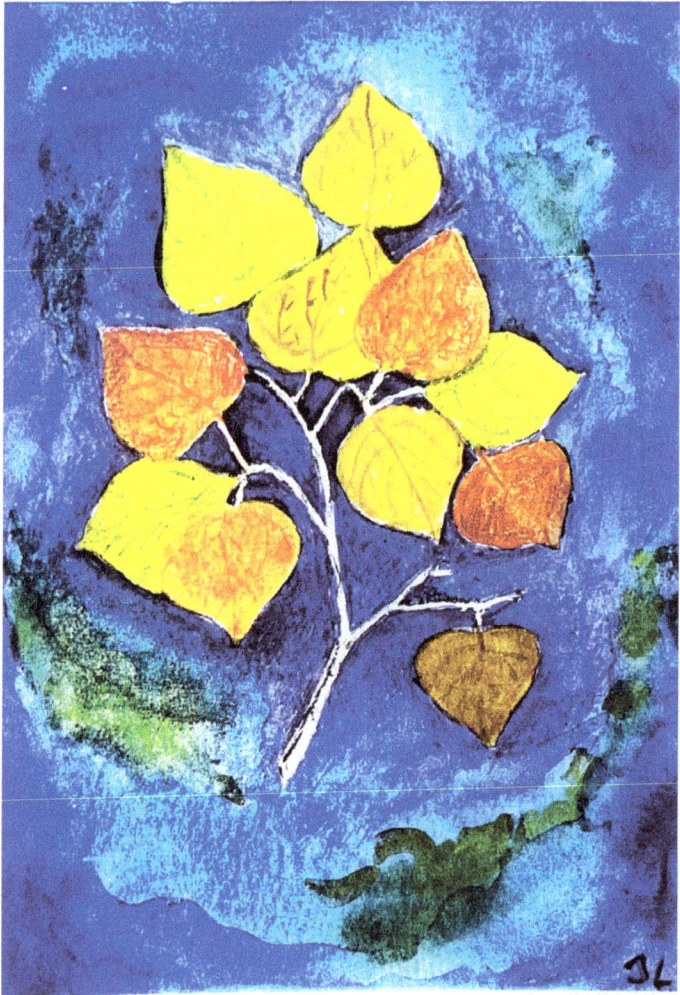

Aspen Gold

From the Editor

Jony Larrowe is someone I never met. I knew her son and his wife, and knew only that he had a sister, Christie, and a brother, Hap.

I first viewed some of these poems on social media, shared by Jony's son Greg after his mother passed away in 2023. Several poems were handwritten by Jony, many accompanied by printed versions published in the *Denver Post, Mountain Gazette, Unity Magazine, Roundup,* and others, some including the dates they were written or published. The earliest date we found on a clipping was 1956.

A truly remarkable woman, Jony speaks of many things unsaid. The poems are filled with humor and are sensitive, thoughtful, honest, and broad in scope, ranging from ski days to romances, from solo hikes to observations on wildlife, from travel with friends and family to dreams that she was a redhead, and much more that caught my attention—so much and so deeply felt.

Jony also kept several books of her art, produced with the same joy and love of this valley. She painted almost daily from her home studio while gazing at the mountains she loved.

I knew I needed to help make her works into a book. These are a few of her poems, paired up with paintings, for Jony's many friends. We created an unusual addition to the appendix of the book—which we call "Jony's Last Word." We hope you enjoy it.

Marjorie DeLuca, Editor

The Naturalist

Winter Alchemy

Apprehensively,
the aspen leaves take part
in autumn's tribal rite.
Each trembling golden heart
quakes through its dance of death
before long winter's night.

And like a treasure store,
the fallen coinage lies,
spent on the forest floor
beneath wild winter skies.

And then…alchemy
mysteriously takes hold.
Leaf-replenished earth
replaces autumn gold.
And riches wrapped in winter's cloak
insure springtime's rebirth.

—*Jony Larrowe*

Case Dismissed

A single stem of lacy wild oats,
one robust red clover blossom,
a stalk of lime-yellow sulphur flower
and a solitary wild rose
blooming ahead of its pink sister buds,
these I mindfully,
carefully picked,
Your Honor…

as well as one penstemon,
blue as angel eyes,
a sun-centered purple aster,
a lavender lupine.
A mere seven stems,
Your Honor.

Yes, I'm guilty,
caught red-handed, or rather
flower-fisted
as I wandered down the mountain trail.
But Your Honor!

I desperately needed these
seven samples of high-country abundance
in order to study them, to love them,
and to paint a watercolor
so that in some future cold and snowy time

I could recall the beauty
and share it with others
who also remember
the joy of wildflower summers.
Guilty, Your Honor.

—*Jony Larrowe*

Lover Bird

A half-cocked robin,
his forehead clownish high,
awaits our car's approach,
a crazed look in his eye.

He hops in frenzied lust
on one foot, then the other,
as I drive into the carport,
turn off the rumbling motor.

He's waiting for his lady-love,
his mimic paramour
who squawks and pipes with passion,
reflecting his ardor.

The shiny rear-view mirror
on the driver's side
is the object of his affection—
his mirror-image bride.

In his wild excitement
this lovesick troubadour
drops ribbons of whitewash
all over our car door,

Confused, this cuckoo robin
who has no real life missus
makes love to his reflection.
He's a LoonyTune Narcissus.

—Jony Larrowe

Song of a Greenhorn

Reap me a tumbleweed harvest.
Fan up a hot desert breeze.
Show me arroyos and alkali flats
guarded by Joshua trees.

Sing me a song of red sunsets
as we lead our horses to drink.
Point out the stars in this blue denim sky.
I'm a frustrated cowboy, I think.

Take me along on a roundup.
Croon me a lonesome old tune.
I'll rustle up some black coffee
while you lasso that high riding moon.

After our night watch is over
let's rise with a stretch and a yawn.
We'll saddle Ole Paint and the mustang
and give chase to a wild-western dawn.

—*Jony Larrowe*

Ap1/'07

Winter Song

Dark spired, silent forests,
a fire opal sky
mirrored in each icicle,
the waning sun's red eye.

December pins ice diamonds
upon each mountain breast
while blasts of wind-blown snow
fly pennants from each crest.

Below the frozen surfaces
of ice-clad alpine streams,
the muffled sounds of water
flow through our winter dreams
And bring to you cold comfort…yet
a song of inner knowing
that spring will soon come dancing in
as soon as it stops snowing.

—Jony Larrowe

Desert Challenge

Show me the great western desert
where lovesick coyotes wail.
Lead me to hazy blue mountains
at the end of a prickly pear trail.

Take me where wild mustangs breed.
Protect me from sidewinder snakes.
As I follow your brave and bold lead,
prove that you have "what it takes!"

Show me hot sands and arroyos
where ghosts of Apaches still loom.
Let sweet-scented night-blooming Cereus
drown us in desert perfume.

Point out "our star" in the heavens,
please! Build us a safe night's barrage.
Then, cuddle with me until sunrise
and swear that it's not…
a mirage.

—Jony Larrowe

CANYON LAND , Colorado JL

Three Haiku

Chickadees and jays
feeding at their breakfast tray—
our morning delight!

The ancient willow
sighs and drops its golden load,
resting up 'til spring.

Luncheon on the deck—
an uninvited hornet…
The party's over!

—Jony Larrowe

OLD MUSIC TENT · ASPEN · CO.

The Poet-Artist

Contrasts

Sometimes I compare ski tracks
with contrails in the air:
High vapor, blue sky
And a plane's white path.

Below, on Earth's bright canvas
ski trails, blue on white
trace through powder snow.

Free-drawn lines etched
across vast clean spaces.
Two-color art,
a passing poem.
I see it and pause,
waiting for the words.

—*Jony Larrowe*

On Rejects...With Determination

To serve my art
I must remorseless be.
Cut, revise and then
throw out
what isn't truly me!

If truth is what
I seek
and clear philosophy,
out with words that
muddle thoughts
before they smother me!

When rejects
cost me stamps and time
and downright
misery...
I'll never let them come
between
the faith I have
in me!

—*Jony Larrowe*

"By some inner mystic
Presence, I was told
To Live and to Love
To Laugh and be Glad"

E. Holmes

JL 4/7/19

I Receive the River

I receive the river.
Ripples tease my skin,
whirlpools spin circles
around my breasts
and all my openings gape,
awaiting the thrust of white water.

The river blood,
scouring my bones,
seeking hidden chambers,
places for crashing cataracts
to drop me deaf and drowning,
drowning until my still-water voice cries.

Oh river Love,
course through me,
your newest channel
flowing.

—*Jony Larrowe*

Epitome   – 1956

Epitome of winter skills
To etch a track in
powder snow
To skim down ~~breathlessly~~
steep ~~hills~~ hills
Then, read the message
from below.

Epitome

Epitome of skiing thrills;
To skim the virgin powder snow,
To trace a pattern down steep hills
Then read its message from below!

         Jony Poschman
         Aspen, Colo.

Denver Post

Family

Family Pet

Not docile nor sweet,
this parakeet…
pugilistic,
ear-tweaking sadistic,
he spars before a mirror
in his cage
then starts attacking seed pods
in blue-bolt lightning rage.

Impaling us with gimlet eyes,
jet bright,
he dares us to infringe upon
his right
to rule his roost
and everyone in sight.

Pompously absurd,
he whistles for attention
then crows a self-love litany—
"Oh pretty, pretty bird!"

—*Jony Larrowe*

This Sea...This Day

Sea children
age-gap forgotten
spanning the distance between
here and whatever's beyond
in the carefree certainty of
Now.

How free their mood!
How bright their day!
What secret wisdom informs them
about the magic of this time,
the foreverness of this
shining sea…
this perfect
Now?

—*Jony Larrowe*

La Jolla, CA.

33

Grandma
Wolf.
5/22/'0

For Christie

My beloved child with broken heart,
your grief, rebellious, growing with each tear,
is such a total thing.

In your hand you hold your lifeless bird
chosen, loved and taught by you this year.
No longer will he sing.

Crumpled ashen feathers in your palm
faded, his blue brilliance, his eyes no longer bright.
Too sudden, his dying!

Tenderly you bury him beneath this tree
and scatter daisies on the tiny mound,
a small girl crying.

Quietly I take your hand…we go,
remembering his jaunty blue-flashed joy.
So real, your sorrow.

Small consolation now, to know
because these are your springtime years.
You'll smile again tomorrow.

—*Jony Larrowe*

To
Christmas Love and
2021 Blessings!

One long ago Christmas
Eve, Peter and I looked out
our bedroom window and
saw a strange little donkey
patiently standing in our
garden its bowed head
covered with snow.
    We joyously tapped at the
window but it didn't look
up. It just stood there,
creating an unforgettable
Christmas scene forever
etched in our hearts;
a special holiday
Blessing! ♥ Tony

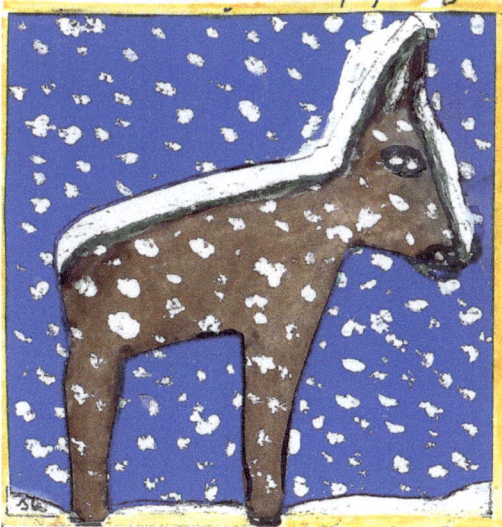

Discovery — 1956

I used to climb the water tower
And dreaming up there by the hour
The fateful apple I would be
Daring you to come to me.

I'd chant some secret woman-song
Of love and hate and right and wrong
And when you came, O breathless
start!
In vain I'd try to still my
heart.

You challenged me, no word was said
Your green eyes taunted me instead
Pretending not to understand
I watched you climb, hand over hand

You swarmed my tower, rung by rung
Strange sweetness rising to your
tongue
And when you saw my face you
knew
That I found first-love tasty, too!

Love

The Ski Instructor
Or…After the Ball Is Over

When she thinks of their together times,
skiing wide, open, ballroom slopes,
or better still—
kicking up powder diamonds
in the dazzle
of a sun-sliced aspen grove,
her heart smiles.

"Follow me!" he calls, cutting tracks before her.
Together they laughed,
braving capricious high-country elements.
Nothing stopped their quest for more and more!
Climbing with skins, plunging down-mountain to
wine picnics, snowball tussles, face plants,
and standing in a whirl of storm-flung flakes,
bear-hugging in steamy closeness.

Then in the early-shadows time,
when the slanting sun slides behind the ridge,
It was "Your place or mine?"
And the fast descent
to her home, hearth…and bed.

Later, she skips a breath
"Tomorrow, same time"
on his way out…to meet the guys?

A new client?
A late date?
She grins agreement, conceding his freedom,
concealing her loss.
And her heart aches for answers.

—Jony Larrowe

Jony and Harry in Tijuana for honeymoon.

The Inglorious Tryst

Soaked by salt spray
we rowed to the island,
to your secret hideaway,
shrouded in morning mist
until the rising Baja sun
blasted wide open,
splashing our world orange.

Flying fish spun rainbow arcs.
Curious baby seals butted our boat ashore.
We burned our bare feet on scorching sand,
following a faint trail that led to your lair.

Beneath the blue-fingered shade of a palm
we folded ourselves down…hot, sweating
and leaning on our elbows,
we sipped warm Tecate, sucking limes
and idly swatting flies.

"Well, here we are," you said.
"Cool," I replied.
Now and then, between sips,
we caught each other's eyes
but we could read
no promises.

It was that kind of a day,

—*Jony Larrowe*

Love Letter

We have sailed wild seas together
and we have plumbed each other's dreams before,
If separation should hover,
parting us one from the other,
it won't be forever more.

We'll merge again…Where? When?
A magic place? Outer space?
And when we do,
together we will spend this love
I hold in trust
for you.

—Jony Larrowe

Cabin at foot of W. Independence Pass.

Sometimes

Sometimes when we're alone together
I watch you thinking to yourself.
I receive your silent words and say them aloud.
And when you vent my inner feelings,
even before I spill them out,
I think I know what soulmates are all about.

Sometimes in public places
when we sit together laughing,
and our joy spins a golden cocoon,
enveloping us, protecting us,
from intrusions other than
our own absurd humor,

I see wistfulness in the eyes of onlookers.
Sometimes we reach out to them,
invite them to share our laughter.

They look away,
bashful, hesitant to acknowledge
our overture.
Sometimes there are others
who welcome our inclusiveness, who
pull up a chair and join us.
"We thought you'd never ask!"

Our space expands, the enchanted circle
contracts in and out like breathing.
We plumb our depths and heights,
the worst and best of our moods, whims, dreams.

Sometimes we think we've discovered
what soulmates are all about.

—Jony Larrowe

Four Haiku

Hush! Softly the snow
envelops our winter dreams,
sighing a lullaby.

Ancient olive trees,
marble nymphs, glowing fireflies…
Italian garden.

Cool caves abandoned,
keening bats stitch the night sky…
moths on the menu!

Shine, wild gypsy moon!
Dancers whirl gaudy colors
Conduct it, Verdi!

—Jony Larrowe

Sopris + Crystal River   2001

Reflections

Being There Then

It was a social thing—
standing in lift lines,
squinting in sun-dazzle,
sliding skis back and forth,
chatting wit h friends,
grasping, leaning on poles,
flexing knees, testing tendons
against the grip of boots and bindings.
The joy of just being there!

Then, riding up and up,
looking deep into white winter,
absorbing the auuum of humming cables,
punctuated by shouts of skiers
exultant in parrot colors,
whipping up powder contrails,
faces frozen into bliss.
The tonic of being there!

Ski talk…with your partner—
Which run to choose?
What wax do you use?
Better yet, no talk.

Imagining being up there,
shoving off into a steep fall-line,
plunging down against the wind,
with sweet,
smooth
powder turns.

The bliss of being there!

—*Jony Larrowe*

Reflections

During my teenage years,
when frequent dramas
and tears
were quite predictable,
I felt that life was so hard,
and, often, quite despicable.

I despaired about my looks…
my hair, my legs, my nose!
All wrong!
And zits on my face!
Oh God! I'm a disgrace!

Today I can smile
at those adolescent agonies.
No longer reflecting moody youth,
the mirror speaks.
I've come of age,
and I accept the truth.

I can contemplate my girth
(it's been with me since birth)
and know that
svelte I'll never be.
But since when is it a sin
to just be me?

A quick look at my knees...
at this late date,
it's not my fate to be
a beauty queen...
but they're pain-free and dependable
and praise be,
bendable!

And then there's impatience
with myself and others.
I'm working on it
and will probably never win,
but still...I'm better than
I've been!

So...throughout
these golden years
I've learned to take
what I've been given
and make the best of it.
To enjoy life...all the rest of it!

—Jony Larrowe

Wild Strawberries

New thoughts
like wild strawberries
reach…stretch red runners,
explore new places.

Tentatively,
an inquiring root
dares to grow
new fruit.

—Jony Larrowe

From my office window —

Request

Let me hold secret this place
where crystal falls
and ferns and moss embrace.
Where rooted in an amber pond
a patriarchal stump holds high
with silvered limbs
a monks-hood clump...
reaching for the sky.

Let me hold secret
this partial-night place
where sun splinters fraction
the midsummer light
upon the forest's face.

Let no one find me here,
This one day let me own
this place...
alone.

—*Jony Larrowe*

Appendix

My Mother's Exceptional Life

Born Jane Elizabeth Purchard in Pittsburgh, Pennsylvania, on July 8, 1926, Jony (pronounced "Johnny") moved with her family to Denver in the 1930s and discovered a lifelong love of the mountains. Her parents were Swiss emigrés. Dr. Dora Purchard was a counselor and psychology professor at Denver University; Paul Purchard, was a mechanical engineer, inventor and patent attorney who helped design Aspen's first chairlift.

At age 16 Jony worked in a Denver ski shop. On weekends she took the ski train to Winter Park, sacrificing lunch money to buy an extra day's ski ticket. She followed famous Swiss skiing legend Fred Iselin with puppy-like enthusiasm and became an expert powder skier. She recounted that Fred would sit her down and insist on watching her eat the lunches he bought for her, after realizing she would starve herself to ski.

At the University of Colorado in Boulder during World War II she would beg off from compulsory bridge games, then she would rappel from the top floor window of the sorority house to join friends from the Colorado Mountain Club for outings. By the mid-1940s she had climbed 22 of Colorado's 14,000-foot peaks. "All the most difficult ones, including our Elk Range!" she said.

She took off the winter of 1945 from college to ski and wait tables at the Alta Lodge. Soon she noticed a former 10th Mountain Ski Trooper named Harry Poschman and quipped to her fellow waitress, "I'll take that one!" When they announced their engagement, Jony's mother feared that she was losing her daughter to a ski-bum lifestyle. They married in 1947, and after anxiously watching their itinerary in sleepy ski resorts like Alta, Sun Valley, and Big Bear, her mother was relieved when they chose the budding cultural center of Aspen, commenting, "In 1949, it was the only ski town with a future."

Jony and Harry moved to Aspen in August 1950, promptly rented an old Victorian house on Main Street, opened a bed-and-breakfast hostel for skiers, and named it after her favorite Swiss alpine flower, edelweiss. Revenue from their Edelweiss Inn, Harry's ski instructing, harvesting potatoes on Woody Creek farms, and construction work on No. 1 chairlift gave them the wherewithal to start a family. They also supplemented their income with foraging, hunting, and fishing—not for sport, but for food.

Jony and her friends raised their children together, taking turns babysitting and skiing. They started the lemonade stand at the Aspen Music Festival tent to raise the salary for a kindergarten teacher. They organized the school carnivals, put on potlucks and ski picnics, and enjoyed the small town life of Aspen in the 50s and 60s.

An avid adventurer, Jony drove her classic Willys Jeep all over the Colorado mountains searching for old mining camps and fields of wildflowers. Along the way she wrote and photographed lifestyle and food columns for the *Aspen Illustrated News*, *The Aspen Times*, and *Snowmass Sun*, published a cookbook, worked as a commercial photographer and illustrator, catered parties and taught cooking classes at Colorado Mountain College.

After a divorce in 1970, Jony rented out rooms in her Waters Avenue home to many people who still live in Aspen today, becoming a surrogate mom to several young seasonal "ski bums" who became locals and lifelong friends.

In 1974 Jony married Peter Larrowe, a World War II veteran and former Trappist monk who had helped build the Snowmass Monastery. They moved to Snowmass Village in 1977, then retired to El Jebel in 1993, where she lived for the rest of her life.

Jony led an active social life, and for well over a decade was a proud member of the Aspen Ladies Literary Society, Aspen's oldest and longest-lasting social club whose members include descendants of pioneers from the mining days. In her final years she enjoyed her circle of good friends at an informal Sunday breakfast group in Basalt.

She passed away on February 14, 2023. Jony will be remembered for her good cheer and compassion for others. She lived the principles of optimism, kindness and generosity.

—*Greg Poschman*

Loving Memories

Her life was full of grace and gratitude. She was a true innocent, a humble teacher who never would take any accolades offered, although she made art every day, and was a wonderful cook and hostess. In her youth, she was an accomplished mountaineer and powder skier.

Through her life she sent thousands of homemade greeting cards but only for the purpose of cheering people up. She also hand-painted china and made enamel-on-copper jewelry that she sold at Alpine Jewelers. She crocheted over a hundred colorful afghans for friends and new parents.

An accomplished writer, she documented many aspects of family history and wrote fiction as well. She wrote photo essays for *Aspen Illustrated News* and *The Aspen Times*, and catered home-cooked meals for events for local hostesses' dinner parties.

A woman of high energy, she would take to the mountains to cheer herself up when she needed an adventure, often with her loving friend Gretl Uhl. I could never mention a Colorado back road or ghost town that she hadn't explored.

She had two long successful marriages. One with my father Harry Poschman whose love of skiing brought them to Aspen in 1950, and one with Peter Larrowe who had been an original monk at the Trappist monastery in Snowmass. For 40 years they traveled the world together.

As a parent, she was permissive, encouraging our individual gifts and proudly showing us off. She and my father believed that travel was the greatest education, so we were regularly whisked out of school to go to the beach and occasionally on bigger trips to Europe.

Surrounded by family, some of her last words were "I'm ready to go lie down in a bed of flowers."

—*Christie Poschman Interlante*

Jony's Last Word

66 It all started when, at age eleven,
I wrote a Christmas poem for my father.
It wasn't so much his praise that elated me
but the joyous feeling of creating something original
that hooked me into writing…and I never stopped!…

I've written for newspapers, magazines,
and there's a whole bunch of journals
in my study…but no collection of poems.
Among [these]…are poems written and sold
in the 1950s. Newer ones [since 2004] were edited
and re-written just yesterday.

Nothing fancy…just everyday images and thoughts
that anyone could experience. 99

Scan this link with your
cell phone, and Christie
and I will sing you some
favorite songs!

Time Pieces

Stunning,
the cream-pearl moon,
displayed with jeweler's cunning
against black velvet sky.

Regal,
heaven's time piece,
with omniscient pride,
measures cyclic crestings
and ebbs of tide.

Faithful,
a pale, enduring clock
chimes each hour,
marks fleeting time
in earth-bound tower.

Steadfast,
it ticks, it tocks,
oblivious of Man's cry…
Oh moon! Oh clock!
How much more time
have I?

—*Jony Larrowe*

One of my poems — perhaps my favorite most of all! Written in late 1950s. Aspe Inspired by a solo hour on the Roaring Fork River.

– mystery –   1963

My soul lies steeping
In the sun
My body, fused to
sun-warmed stone ....
The sun, the stone,
my soul are One
Yet three-in-one
I lie alone!

Sun Worship

My soul lies steeping in the sun
My body fused to sun-warm stone,
The song of sky and stream is one
In breathless trance
I lie alone.

And yet, how can one be withdrawn
From nature's pure and holy song?
The sun, the stone and stream chant on
In tune with them
I sing along.

Sept. 1, 1957   *Jonni Poschman*
                        Aspen, Colo.

Denver Post

www.ingramcontent.com/pod-product-compliance
Lightning Source LLC
Chambersburg PA
CBHW051300020426
42333CB00026B/3287